A Dreamer's Mind

A Dreamer's Mind

A Collection of Motivational Poetry

RYAN WILSON

publishedbyryanwilson@gmail.com
ISBN-13: 9781729422366

www.instagram.com/wilsonryan__

A Dreamer's Mind: A Collection of Motivational Poetry

"Always bear in mind that your own resolution to succeed is more important than any other one thing."

—Abraham Lincoln

DEDICATION

To my mom, Anne.
Thank you for the strength, support and wisdom.

TABLE OF CONTENTS

PREFACE

The predominantly free verse-style poems expressed in this collection are meant to be read in essentially any tone or progression, just so long as the words are interpreted in a *positive* manner and context.

Words are powerful in that they are expressive, and perhaps even more so when they are impactful. If my words are to serve one purpose beyond just my expression, that is to have an entirely positive impact.

The appreciation that I feel in being able to compose these works and share them is not taken for granted.

Thank you, and enjoy!

PART I

MEANT FOR ME

Meant for Me

What is meant to be,
will surely manifest.
And no sooner,
than at the perfect time.

LOSE OR WIN

Lose or Win

If you fail to win,
you still have not lost.
The lesson begins,
when the win falls short.
It will only be a failure,
at the expense of the lesson.
If the knowledge is not captured,
the failure solidifies.
When the wisdom is secured,
success will manifest.
The defeats harness power,
greater than victory.
With every loss,
is the *opportunity* to learn.
The moment you have lost,
is the moment you will have become victorious.

A DEDICATION

A Dedication

To be *dedicated*,
and *determined*.
Is to be,
disciplined.
Three forces,
powerfully balanced.
A triangular foundation,
together in unison.
The absence of one,
causes the others to fall.
All three in consistency,
or all three are compromised.

MIND BODY SOUL

Mind Body Soul

Manifesting is maximized,
when entire power is harnessed.
Hitting your stride,
to fire on all cylinders.
That is to provide power,
on all three levels of your being.
The *mind*,
with the *body*.
Both combined,
with the *soul*.
The intentions of one,
leave lasting effects on all.
Direct the trio together,
or the power to lead is forfeited.
A balance of powers,
equipped with cohesive energy sources.
Fuel all three in consistency,
or suffer from compromise.

PART II

RISE AND SHINE

Rise and Shine

In adverse times of life
it can seem like the darkness is never-ending.
But a new day is coming
and often times it is closer than we even realize.
The night is darkest in the moments
directly prior to the arrival of dawn.
Just as it seems like circumstances can't get worse
a new day finally arrives.
And just like the sun
we *rise*.

Rise and *Shine*

When life creates a storm
it can seem like the rain is going to last forever.
It may be pouring harder than ever
but the rain will eventually cease.
As the clouds clear away
the sun begins to emerge.
Now is the time
the time to truly shine.
Keep walking through the storm
as it will not rain forever.
When the storm passes
the skies will clear.
The shine will be powerful
and naturally profound.
Endure the storm
until it is time to *shine*.

LOCK IN AND LEVEL UP

Lock in and Level up.

To be great,
it might be essential.
Zone in.
Tap into yourself.
The noise that lies beyond your zone is silenced.
It is nonexistent.
True power.
Focus.
To be great,
it might be essential.
Lock in.

Lock in and *Level up*

To be great,
it will be imperative.
Your next move,
will be your best move.
Settle for nothing.
Aspire for everything.
To be great,
it will be imperative.
Level up.

PART III

WALK YOUR OWN PATH /
THE ANSWERS WITHIN
PARTS I AND II

Walk Your Own Path / The Answers Within
Part I

Follow your path,
break free from the crowd.

Listen to yourself,
take heed of your own instincts.

The answers are there,
often deep within.

Be sure to tune in,
careful and close.

The voice of your soul,
is sometimes quiet and slight.

It has never been wrong,
it will always be right.

Walk Your Own Path / The Answers Within
Part II

The voice of the crowd,
screams loud and it's hoarse.

Perhaps they know best,
but your path is compelling.

Your soul will guide you,
while the crowd will control you.

Greatness is yours,
it is embedded within you.

While the crowd may go left,
you shall proceed right.

At first it may seem different,
but that is quite alright.

GRAY / EQUALITY

Gray / Equality

Gray is balance,
which will always feel right.

Gray embodies equality,
between black and the white.

It is never too dark,
nor is it too light.

Gray represents equality,
within human life.

Only by collaboration,
can the powers unite.

Like the sun without rain,
or a day without night.

A universe missing balance,
will never feel right.

Balance and equality,
create beauty and shine bright.

Gray equals balance,
like a spark ready to ignite.

Gray is equality,
and a fire we have no choice but to light.

PART IV

PRICELESS DREAMS

Priceless Dreams

As soon as you realize that you're after more than just
money,
is the moment that everything that you're working
towards, will move closer to becoming reality.
In order to attain the life that you seek, you have to first
learn that your purpose
is beyond just money. Start being productive, and working towards living out *dreams*.
Instead of just searching for a way to be *rich*. Develop and
set goals, and work positively towards achieving them.
The money and the success, will come naturally. Find
yourself and your purpose first,
and then you will be ready to receive all that life has for
you.
Spend time chasing your dreams,
and the money will end up chasing you.

COMFORT ZONES

Comfort Zones

There lies value and purpose,
beyond your boundaries.

To step outside
of your comfort zone.
        Taking strides towards something
        that may be unfamiliar or uncertain.
            Life will reward you
            with new opportunities.
                Life will provide new experiences
                and *blessings.*
                    Staying with what feels comfortable
                    only to avoid change?
                        That can put a limit
                        or a ceiling on your greatness.

                        The further that you expand
                        your comfort zone,
                        the further your dreams will go.

PART V

BLACKBIRD

blackbird

Fly high,
at peace with all of my pride.
Not a shriek not a cry,
that's forever my reply.
Cloak dark as black,
and they always react.
In their world they stay far,
but my mindset is unmatched.
The alike are aware,
the crowds keep distance.
Strictly follow instincts,
and be simply idealistic.
Fly slow,
and live fast.
Always in the moment,
despite the years passed.
Eyes forever forward,
and patient with time.
Fly high on the ground,
thoughts way up in the sky.
A blackbird's light,
shines in the darkest of nights.

MY MOMENT

My Moment

Exist in the moment
or suffer from yesterday.
Exist in the moment
or squander tomorrow.
The moment is all,
the moment is life.
The moment is the struggle.
The moment is success.
It is all that we truly have.
It is all that we truly need.
Enjoy this, right here.
Take it all in.
Enjoy it!
Stay in the moment.

ACTION

Action

Go get it.
Act.
Live.
Learn.
Smile!
Laugh.
Exist.
Excel.
Live!
Go get it.

ABOUT THE AUTHOR

Ryan Wilson is a young writer from the East Coast of the United States who has been studying and practicing the law of attraction for more than six years. Ryan has a Bachelor of Science degree and combines a spiritual approach with his business and sports backgrounds to spread the ideas of success. In the time spent analyzing and learning the ways of the universe through manifestation and positive energy, Ryan made it a goal of his to spread motivation and positivity to others. As his journey continues, he is willing to lead the way for anyone chasing their dreams.

You can follow Ryan Wilson on Instagram-
@wilsonryan__

Made in the USA
Middletown, DE
19 November 2018